D1553232

A LIFE SHARED

Meaningful Conversations With Our Kids

ELLEN MARTIN

WITH SHARON BRYANT, LMFT, RPT

FIRST EDITION

ISBN: 978-1-946466-26-6

Library of Congress Control Number: 2017958116

Published by

P.O. Box 2839, Apopka, FL 32704

Printed in the United States of America

Disclaimer: The views and opinions expressed in this book are solely those of the author and other contributors. These views and opinions do not necessarily represent those of Certa Publishing. Please note that Certa Publishing's publishing style capitalizes certain pronouns in Scripture that refer to the Father, Son, and Holy Spirit, and may differ from some publishers' styles.

What others are saying about...

A LIFE SHARED

Ibelieve Ellen Martin has written a tremendously helpful tool both for parents and those positioned to help them—clinicians, pastors, and others. She shows parents how they can share life with their children in a way that incorporates knowledge-based principles in combination with faith in a down-to-earth style any parent can grasp. When I need parenting advice, I call Ellen! I genuinely believe others can benefit from her wisdom and experience too.

Sharon Bryant
Licensed Marriage Family Therapist
Registered Play Therapist

In a distracted age, when smartphones and screens are ripping at the fabric of family life, *A Life Shared* reminds parents there is nothing more priceless we can offer our children than the gift of conversation itself. Born out of her love for Christ and the family, and flowing out of her own rich experience as a mother, Ellen Martin, invites us to discover and develop the art of conversation with our children. Written in an engaging, down-to-earth way, rooted in deep wisdom, and packed with real-life examples, here is a book that will both instruct you how and inspire you to do it. I believe reading it will change you and your family.

Stephen A. Seamands, PhD
Professor of Christian Doctrine
Asbury Theological Seminary

———————— 🦋 ————————

As a pastor and denominational executive, I know churches seek resources that speak to families. *A Life Shared* uses conversation to draw people together and build supportive relationships between parents and children, networks of parents, and each of us and the God who parents us. It recognizes the uniqueness of each family, and acknowledges our universal longing for meaningful connection with one another. In an increasingly fragmented and rushed world, Ellen reminds us how to form deep, lasting relationships with those we love most.

Rev. Amy R. Wagner
Director of Congregational
Development & Revitalization
Western Pennsylvania Conference
of the United Methodist Church

———————— 🦋 ————————

Ellen Martin has hit the mark with a concise, wise MUST READ for all parents. As a licensed pastoral counselor, play therapist and spiritual director, my days are spent listening to pains from childhood or current life. Most often, these hurts are relational. When I read this manuscript, I was overjoyed to have a real-life approach to communication to share with my clients. *A Life Shared* invites parents to take one small step toward reaching the hearts and souls of their children through everyday conversation. I can only imagine the homes that will be more peaceful, full of joy and laughter, and love after this read.

Kathy Milans
Licensed Pastoral Counselor
Registered Play Therapist-Supervisor
Spiritual Director

———————— ❧ ————————

A Life Shared by Ellen Martin is a gift. She shares from her experience as a daughter and a mother of having life-shaping conversations that give depth and fabric to our most crucial relationships. She is not perfect, but her authenticity is disarming. She does not lecture, but rather gives practical advice that helps nurture healthy communication. She does not just name the challenges, but gives practical suggestions to help even the busiest of parents to disengage from what is less important—and reengage in what is most important. I highly recommend this book.

Jeff Greenway
Lead Pastor of the Reynoldsburg
United Methodist Church

———————— ❧ ————————

Parents are desperate for meaningful ways to connect with their kids, secretly hoping the church will fill in the gaps and address sticky issues. Ellen Martin builds a bridge between biblical foundations, good theology, and everyday conversations of adults and children. She is not offering a free bag of tricks, but an authentic approach to doing life together as families.

Ellen L. Marmon, PhD
Professor of Christian Discipleship
Asbury Theological Seminary

With this book, Ellen Martin has given us a gift if we will only receive it. Our parenting is too often a passive reaction to life's busyness rather than an active attentiveness to the daily opportunities God gives us through our children. Her gentle, practical proposal of "meaningful conversations" leads us to recognize with greater wonder the image of God in our sons and daughters, and to realize anew that just when we think we are forming them, they are really teaching us. I endorse her book as an excellent resource for parents, families, parishes, small groups, and all faith communities.

Mike Allen, M. Div., D. Min.
Director of Family Life and Evangelization
Catholic Diocese of Lexington, KY

To my husband, kids, and all of my parents.

I live a life shared better because of you.

Acknowledgements

This book stands on a long history of others calling me to write and those who made this book possible. These are not acknowledgments, but heartfelt gratitude.

A high school teacher first encouraged my writing. Reg Johnson told me I was a writer as he handed me my first graded seminary paper. My dear friend Melissa Lowe recommended me for a piece that became my first article and is now a workshop. Kathy Milans continued the opportunity for me to write when she invited me to write my first parenting article. If it had not been for Katie Moore, I would have never accepted that invitation. Andrew Dragos invited me to submit articles to Seedbed at my convenience, and Patricia Taylor echoed their celebration of my 800-1200-word submissions.

Mothering filled my days more and more. I wrote less and less. As I mothered, people encouraged me to write. Friends, strangers, church members, and family. I prayed, mothered the boys, and assumed I would write when they grew up and moved out.

Then this book began to spring forth. A few notes here and

there turned into a full outline. Conversations with some dear friends, my husband, Ellen Marmon, Cathy Stonehouse, and Kathy Milans helped me embrace the ideas as a book. Thank you, community.

Amanda Reifsynder read the introduction and first three chapters. I needed a cheerleader, an assurance that I was saying something. She played the part well. Thank you, dear friend.

Parents and children shared their stories to make this book richer. Each one invited me into sacred space. Thank you. You know your names.

Without Angel Crowell, this book would have never become reality. She took calls from me late at night when I was stuck. She read every chapter and offered insightful feedback. She pushed me when I needed it. She cheered me on too. Thank you, "editor" supreme.

Sharon Bryant made this book complete. Her skills and resources complemented mine. I had called her as a friend and therapist wanting feedback. She became a collaborator. I hope this is the first of many books we work on together. Thank you, dear friend.

There are many who have rejoiced over this work and cheered me along the way. If you ever listened to me talk about this book for than five minutes, you are one of those. Thank you.

Certa Publishing allowed this book to see the light of day. You are many answers to many prayers. Thank you, Patrick, Sheila, and Jennifer.

Stephanie Beeken, Sue Elam, Sandy Elam, and Sherry Ferrell. There are no words to express your part in this. I trust you know my gratitude runs deeper than deep for your love and support.

Andrew and the boys. In so many ways, they are this

10

book. They prayed for me and the book, ate cereal more than ever before, lived in an increasingly dirty home, read parts here and there, asked about it often, and did it all gladly. The number of nights my husband put the kids to bed alone, so I could write, were many. You are my life shared.

Table Of Contents

Introduction

They knew something was wrong. I was far too quiet. I had been crying earlier while on the phone.

"What is it, Momma?" the oldest asked.

"I will tell you at dinner," I tenderly explained.

We were seated now. Dinner was served. It was time to answer my son's question.

"You know momma has been crying today." I started. They nodded. "Well, Papaw went to the doctor, and they found something in his body called cancer."

"What's cancer?" one of the boys asked.

"Cancer is something that makes you really sick," I explained.

"Oh. Well, his doctor will give him medicine, and he will be all better," resolved the seven-year-old.

"Cancer is tricky. Sometimes the doctors give you medicine, and you get better. Sometimes you get better for a little while, and then you get sicker. Sometimes the cancer just moves to a different place where it thinks the medicine can't get it. Sometimes the cancer gets mad at the medicine. It throws a tantrum and gets bigger." I paused. "It's scary for him. I might be on the phone a lot more with him. I might be sad sometimes. I just wanted you to know," I explained to our three boys with the baby in my arms. My husband smiled gently and gave a nod of encouragement. We had begun a conversation no one wants to have.

We never planned to have such weighty conversations with our young kids. It just happened. They asked questions, and we answered them. Before our first-born could talk, he would point, and we would name the object of his wonder. When he could talk, he asked questions, "What's this, Momma?"

As he grew older, the questions changed. One day he found a baby bird dead outside our door. It had fallen from the exterior attic vent. It was bloated and naked with sparse wing feathers. My sweet four-year-old son looked at the bird. He looked at me.

"We need to bury it, Momma," he announced.

With a shovel in hand, the bird Bounty®-wrapped and laid in a small box, we walked to a corner of the backyard. My young son asked a question of theologians, "Will the bird live again?"

I thought for a moment. Would the bird live again? The rocks can cry out in praise, Jesus said. Even the animals were spared in the land of Nineveh after repentance. There will be a new heaven and new earth, Jesus promised. All the creatures will be there.

"Yes, the bird will live again. When Jesus comes again, all of life will be resurrected. Those who love Him will be with Him, even this baby bird."

"Will he fly right out of the ground, Momma?" my inquiring first-born asked smiling.

"I don't know, but that sure would be exciting," I replied in awe at his wonder. We buried the bird. We thanked God for the bird and the resurrection of life. We had had a meaningful conversation. A conversation we both remember to this day. It was the first of many. It was the beginning of something greater than we ever expected.

Both my husband and I care for our kids. We feed, clothe, and educate them. We take them to school, martial arts, wrestling, volunteer projects, worship, and youth group week after week. We share the demands of daily life with chores and responsibilities. While we live out the day-to-day activities of parenting, we share life with our kids. We talk about their interests and our interests, their days and our days, their fears and our hope in the one true God. Together as parents and children, we share life. The natural response for us to answer the questions of our young children did more than we could have ever imagined. Their innocent questions and our willing answers deepened our relationships. The conversations wind through the years as a part of our relationship. As our kids grow older, the conversations change and our relationships grow deeper. Deep relationships are rooted in conversation.

We raise our children with the hopes of *a life shared* into their adulthood. I sometimes count down the years when five children will not live under our roof. It seems we have always had children. By our fifth anniversary, we had three. I dream of the time when just my husband and I have our own adventures. I also dream of visits to college campuses, holiday visits with our sons and their own families, and the joys we have yet to know and cannot imagine as parents of adult children. Because we share life with our kids now, I trust they will share their lives with us in years to come. We enjoy them now. We choose each other again and again as we share life—from first crushes to Lego® creations.

We are not friends. I am the mom. I will always be the mom, but one day I will not parent them on a daily basis. I will welcome them home for visits. I will talk with them and text like I do with my parents now. We will be adults who share life with one another because today, we choose to cultivate our relationship through conversation. At least, that's the hope. That's my dream.

But for now, we get food on the table night after night, schoolwork completed, clothes for the next day, and just enough sleep to do it all over again. Life can be hard. Some weeks, just getting everything done feels like more than we can handle. We can live in the same house, yet never *share life* because the demands of life consume us. I know because I have lived life this way. Sometimes I still do. *A Life Shared: Meaningful Conversations with Our Kids* was written to empower parents to make the shift from life *with* our kids, to life *shared* with our kids through conversation.

We will begin with the definition of a *meaningful conversation* and its role in the family. To have a meaningful conversation, parents must realize their role. Our kids look to us to set the stage and tone for our relationship with them. We can invite them into a conversation and share life with them. That is their desire. It is our potential joy. But what does that look like? A conversation with a three-year-old is not the same as one with an eleven-year-old, so we will look at conversation with kids.

Conversation is not easy. That is why there are so many conversation starters and how-to articles on the market. Conversations are lost to the many unrealized obstacles and missed opportunities. Many times we do not know what conversation looks like in a family. Parents want to share life with their kids in ways they never experienced when they were growing up. They want to be open and available but have so many questions. What do we talk with our kids about? What do we not share? What is too much? Where do we begin without examples?

We can empower our kids to have wonderful life experiences, as well as help them navigate through difficult experiences. We can walk with them through disappointment and confusion into victory and rejoicing.

A Life Shared: Meaningful Conversations with Our Kids is conversational by design. It will help you become aware of what to avoid and what to embrace for meaningful conversation. I will share. You will respond. My part is born out of countless mistakes, love chosen again and again, the example of many, and years of prayer that continues today.

A conversation is never complete with the voice of one. Several families have contributed their stories to this book. Some shared their victories. Others shared their redeemed regrets. Along with the families who have shared stories in this book, you have a part—your obstacles, opportunities, victories, and confessions—to share and pray through.

"Your Turn To Share" is space at the end of each chapter for your part in this conversation. I will ask you questions related to each chapter. You get to answer them. Take time to jot down your answers.

"Give It A Try" suggests actions and observations. They may not feel natural, but as the section says, "Give It A Try." Above all, ask God to show you where you need to grow, and where you already thrive. Let Him parent you as you open your heart in reflection, and open yourself to your kids in conversation.

Just as we long to share life with our kids, God longs to share life with us. He sees us and loves us. A willingness to see ourselves as we are takes great courage. It also gives us the opportunity to be made by our good God into the fullness of who He made us to become. We can live life fully and freely when we open our hearts to Him. With our hearts open to Him, we become open to others. We can live *a life shared* through meaningful conversations with one another and our kids.

Jesus, help us live *a life shared*
with You and our kids.

Your Turn To Share

Our kids ask questions, and we answer them. What are some things your kids have asked you? Does a specific conversation come to mind?

What compelled you to read this book? What do you hope to find here?

When you dream of the day your kids are adults, how do you imagine your relationships with them? What kind of conversations will you have with them, how often, and when?

How do you see yourself already moving toward this dream?

What do you need from God for your dream to become a reality?

Give It A Try!

OBSERVE. Watch the rhythm of conversations with your kids. When do they happen? When don't they happen?

OBSERVE. Pay attention to how you respond to the questions your kids ask.

PRAY. Ask God to show you how you already share life with your kids. What are the little things that hinder you from sharing life with your kids?

———————— ❧ ————————

Chapter One

Conversation Defined

In our family, we sometimes have confusion about the meaning of words. I say, "Pick-up your room." They hear, "Shove stuff into the closet and under the bed." So, what is a *meaningful conversation*? According to Webster, conversation is *the act or an instance of talking together.* According to Wikipedia, a conversation is a *form of interactive, spontaneous communication between two or more people. Typically, it occurs in spoken communication.* In this book, a conversation is three things: 1) an exchange between people, 2) a practice, and 3) a foundation for relationship.

A meaningful conversation is different for each person. When a friend calls and you connect so that you lose track of time—that is a meaningful conversation. When you sit down with a parent or spouse and talk about life with one another— that is a meaningful conversation. When your daughter tells you about her dreams, and you stop, listen, and dream with her—that is a meaningful conversation. When you sit on the sidelines or the bleachers while your kid plays ball, and you tell a parent at the end of the game, "It was good to visit,"—that was a meaningful conversation. Meaningful conversations are an exchange between people that invite or enrich relationship as you share life with one another.

Conversation is an exchange between people.

I participate in a book club twice a year. I love the fellowship and comradery I experience. Our time together is one conversation after another. Sometimes the conversations build on one another. One person shares. Another person responds. We may be on page 20 for a while and then flip to page 100. It's often like a wonderful game of word association. One person names a thing; another responds with something it made them think of—and around it goes. We share on a common topic—the book. Somehow it always finds its way into our lives. The voices carry the conversation from something outside of ourselves and a book, to personal places in our minds and hearts. The book club is rich and personal because we had relationships with one another before we started meeting together. We don't get to be together often, so we read a book, gather together, and in those moments, we share life through meaningful conversation.

In our family, dinner is a time to share life. Some nights it is survival of the fittest with five boys, who sometimes forget they have manners. The conversation is anything but meaningful. Other nights, the conversation fills us with laughter and joy. One night, not long ago, I marveled at the conversations at hand. It began with the best way to disguise your kale.

"Take a bite with the roast and mashed potatoes. It's so good. You stack it up on your fork. It's so good," one declared.

"When I'm an adult, I'm going to buy a Christmas tree, ornaments, and drink lots of Monster® soda," the five-year old announced out of nowhere.

"That stuff will kill you," another rebutted. "It's just sugar and caffeine."

Monster® soda led to the excessive amounts of Coke® I drank in undergrad—so much that my eyelids twitched. My husband ran down memory lane and shared a deer-hunting trip with friends from college. Suddenly, our boys were dreaming of visits home from college with friends and the meals I would make for them. I sat back and smiled. It was really nonsense. The conversation went around and around from one thing to the next. There was no focus or point to it at all, but we were together. We enjoyed, remembered, and dreamed life. There were no fights or lectures—just smiles and laughter. It was a meaningful conversation that started with kale.

Conversation is a practice.

Soon after our first child was born, we began to read Bible stories at night. Once he was mobile, it looked and felt like a complete waste of time. One night, I recorded the chaos of reading to a twenty-month-old and a crying infant in my journal.

"Why do we bother?" I prayed.

The very next day our oldest cried out during his play time, "Bow down and worship the statue!"

I laughed out loud. What looked like a disaster was a story in his mind and heart. My son was role-playing as the mighty King Nebuchadnezzar, who sent Shadrach, Meshach, and Abednego to the fire for not worshiping a statue. The practice of reading nightly was not lost. It had only begun. It is the same with meaningful conversation. It does not just happen. It must be practiced. It must be chosen again and again, and then the sweet moment of *a life shared* surprises you with joy.

Some conversations are ongoing. They may not be

meaningful conversations in and of themselves, but they offer us the practice of conversation in our relationship. Our dinner conversations are an established practice. Long ago, we chose to eat dinner together so that we could share our days with one another. When the older kids were young, it felt like survival of the fittest every night. No. It *was* survival of the fittest, but it was our practice. We ate together and shared life through conversation.

Some conversations allow you to develop the practice of conversation in your family. The hobby of bird watching has been that for us. Years ago, my husband hung a little bird feeder by our eat-in kitchen window. Every day we watched the chickadees. Those were our only visitors.

When we moved outside of town, my husband hung a large feeder in front of our living room window. Now, almost daily, we name the birds we have seen at the feeder. Downy, hairy, and red-bellied woodpeckers. Titmice and chickadees. We watch the yellow-finches transform from the winter to summer plumage and back again. We share with one another bird sightings, especially new ones. The juveniles delight us year after year. It's one thing our whole family enjoys. It is not a meaningful conversation, but it is an ongoing conversation that draws us together. It allows us to share a common interest and in turn, strengthens our relationships. The conversation is about birds. While we talk about the birds, we share life with a common interest—a delight in creation, right outside our window.

Conversation is a practice we choose as much as any discipline that shapes our life. We still choose to eat dinner together. It is harder with older kids—between our schedules and theirs—but we choose the practice because it brings life to our family. With our oldest entering the teen years, he is quieter than he used to be while we visit over dinner. But it is our practice and he remains with us at the table. Sometimes he even lingers and joins in the conversation.

When we choose conversation as a practice, two things happen.

1) Conversation becomes part of the family culture—a relational dynamic.
2) Meaningful conversation becomes possible at any time.

For conversation to become part of the family culture—a relational dynamic—we cannot talk *at* our kids. We must listen *to* them and share *with* them. As I have listened to those who have shared their conversations with me, some have said they had conversations, but it was not a regular part of their family. They weren't conversational. Conversations were out of need. Those families walked with their kids through the highs and lows of life, but the day-to-day activities got lost in the shuffle. I understand that all too well. Sometimes the daily responsibilities for taking care of the kids are so great, those meaningful conversations fall off the radar. However, the reality remains. The foundation of relationships is made up of day-to-day conversations that shape our relationships and carry us into the future. The relationship is not limited to the demands of life and parenting. Instead, the parent-child relationship enlarges to include our interest in one another and commitment to share life together.

When we choose conversation as a practice, the meaningful conversation becomes possible at any time. We don't have to pull out the conversation starters and hope for some magical moment. With conversation as a relational dynamic, our kids know we welcome them. They can share something important on their mind. They know we are a safe space to share their heart because we have proven to be genuinely interested in them. The practice of conversation, a true exchange, with our kids today carries our relationship into the future.

Conversation is a foundation for a relationship.

In many ways, I have already begun this point. Isn't that just like a conversation? You get ahead of yourself. Things aren't always clean cut and neat. Sometimes you bounce around. Kids are good at this. Even though kids are not adults, we do have some fundamental similarities. As adults, we are close to those we share our lives with. We turn to those we can trust ourselves with. We seek understanding from those willing to listen to our hearts and answer our questions. This is not unique to adults. It is the same with kids. We all remember meaningful conversations we have had with friends, kids, colleagues, parents, and sometimes, even strangers. When my kids read stories about themselves in this book, they grinned ear to ear and said, "I remember that."

Kids know meaningful conversations when they happen. They have the same need for them as we do. Our kids long to share their lives with us. They trust us and look to us for guidance, or at least know guidance is ours to give to them. They need us to parent them. They also need us to listen to their hearts. They need us to *share* our lives with them.

As parents, we are devoted to our kids. We do so much for them. We make sure they have everything they need, and then some. We love them. They can drive us crazy and then melt our hearts. The relationship is inherent. They are our kids, and we are their parents. The *nature* of the relationship is plain. It is a parent-child relationship. The *quality* of the relationship is more complicated.

My parents did not raise me in the faith. Their marriage ended early, and like all parents they made mistakes. Nonetheless, they shared life with me—openly and honestly—in conversation. I once told my mother, "If I do half the job you did, the boys will turn out alright."

She smiled. "Oh honey, you are twice the mother I was."

When I was in seminary, I realized the relationship I shared with my parents was a treasure. Several classmates raised in Christian homes had strained relationships with their parents. They loved their parents, but they did not enjoy them. Their relationship was sustained only by their family ties. The relationship was complicated. This is a reality many know. Adult children in a relationship with parents where life is not shared end up with disappointment and regret.

Remember our dream as parents? It was to share life with our kids over holidays and college visits and to enjoy visits with them, their spouses, and their kids. This does not just happen. We must choose to make this happen. The dreams we dream are filled with laughter and joy, the fruit of love. Conversation is the key to this dream of *a life shared.*

We choose today to listen to our kids, each one for who they are. We welcome them to share life with us. When we do this again and again, making conversation a practice, they know we value them. Because conversation is never one-sided, we trust them with ourselves as we share our lives and our hopes. They know us—not simply as their parent—but the person we are.

Conversation establishes a foundation for a rewarding parent-child relationship. One day they will grow up and move on, and we won't parent them anymore. The meaningful conversations we have today will make our dreams for *a shared life* reality. When we listen to our kids' hearts and share ourselves with them, we move from an inherent parent-child relationship, to a relationship where we embrace our children out of love.

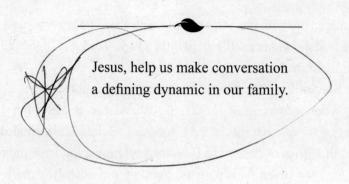

Jesus, help us make conversation
a defining dynamic in our family.

Your Turn To Share

Did you try something in the "Give It A Try" section of the introduction? What did you observe about your family life and conversation? *We don't really have good dynamic conversation*

I define a conversation as an exchange between people, a practice, and a foundation for relationship. What do you think about conversation as a practice and foundation for a relationship?

I shared meaningful conversations from my life. What is a *meaningful conversation* from your life? What made it meaningful?

Take a moment to remember some meaningful conversations with your kids? What effect do you think it had on your relationship? How did it help you share life with your child?

How were conversations a part of your family growing up? What do you want to keep from your childhood conversations? What do you want to be different?

Meaningful conversations don't just happen. You must choose to practice conversations again and again. How could this be difficult for you? What has helped you find victory over other difficult things? What might help you chose conversation as a practice?

Give It A Try!

OBSERVE AND DISCUSS. Notice what your family talks about. Ask your kids what conversations they enjoy in your family.

BRAINSTORM. Bird watching provides a common interest for ongoing conversation in our family. What is something your family has in common? If you can't think of something, brainstorm as a family. Take five minutes or longer to share things you've always wanted to try. You might find a new ongoing conversation.

CREATE SPACE AND PRACTICE. Dinner around the table provides space for conversation in my family. Pick something your family does together that could provide space for conversation. Some ideas are dinner, breakfast, walks, conversation while doing a quiet activity, or errands. Practice conversation, talking with one another as a true exchange, during that time.

OBSERVE AND RESPOND. Notice how much time you talk to your kids and how much time you listen. Have one conversation each day with a child where all you do is listen—no teaching or lecturing. Just listen to your child's heart. After you listen, respond to let them know you heard them.

———— ❧ ————

Chapter Two

Conversation Obstacles, Opportunities, and Challenges

Meaningful conversation is hard. Challenges and obstacles make it even harder. Challenges leave us unsure of how to start. Obstacles are part of life. Opportunities seem few and far between. Because of our busy schedules, it is hard to find time to share our day with one another. Challenges require a different perspective, or they become obstacles. Obstacles can be overcome when we acknowledge them and the messages they send. Opportunities can be found within the obstacles. Then we can have meaningful conversations with our kids.

A Real-Life Scenario

My kids approach me, "Mom."

"Yes, I'm listening," as I finish a text without looking at them.

They talk away. I finish my text and miss every word. I set my phone down and look at them.

"I'm sorry. What did you say?" I confess.

I will not talk with my husband while he texts. I wait until he is done because I know he is not truly listening as his attention is elsewhere. My five- and three-year-old do not yet possess that measure of patience or awareness. Sometimes I invite them to wait patiently. I finish quickly, set my phone down, and give them my full attention. I send powerful messages when I do those three things:

1) You must wait your turn when you want to talk.
2) What you want to say to me is important because you are important to me.
3) I am available to listen to you and respond, even if it takes a moment.

These messages encourage our kids to embrace us as parents.

What do I teach them when I say I'm listening, but I'm not? I teach them at least three things:

1) You can interrupt people and talk at them whenever you want.
2) What you must say is not as important to me as what I am doing.
3) I am not available. I will pretend to listen but hear nothing.

These messages teach our kids they aren't as important to us as our task.

These lessons may seem exaggerated or harsh, but actions speak louder than words. How do you feel when your spouse says to you, "I'm listening" while busy on the phone? How would you feel if the roles with your child were reversed? You need to speak to your child, but she is busy with a screen and only pretends to listen. It is easy to let my kids talk at me while I am on a device and pretend I am listening. It is convenient parenting, but it does not yield *a life shared.*

The messages from conversation obstacles and opportunities are never spoken. They are held within our actions and choices. Actions are powerful because they are subtle and repeated routinely. Our actions ring loud communicating unspoken messages.

"I am not available; I will pretend to listen, but hear nothing."

"I am available to listen and respond, even if it takes a moment."

These messages of rejection or embrace are powerful. The message we express the most tells our kids our desire for relationship. We can choose convenient parenting and all not be lost. Our kids are resilient and extravagantly forgiving. The message we want to send most is, "I am here for you. Share your life with me." When we recognize obstacles and the messages they send, we can create opportunities. Messages of embrace can overcome messages of rejection.

Obstacle: Screen Time

We are products of the age of information. Screens shape our lives from DVDs in our minivans to iPads on our laps. My phone rings and my three-year-old runs for it, hollering, "Your phone, Momma! Your phone!"

Screen time is a daily event whether you limit it to 20 minutes, or leave the TV and computer running 24/7. Life without the internet may be lost forever. Facebook and Pinterest draw us into the screen and away from those present with us. The screens that connect us to the outside world can leave us disconnected and distracted from one another as a family. Without self-awareness and intentional usage, screens are an obstacle to conversation and relationship.

Opportunity: Face Time

After finally admitting some bad habits with screen time, I took a break from Facebook. After just one week, I told my kids that things seemed different with me since being off Facebook. The oldest three replied in quick unison, "Yeah!"

"Is it that different?" I asked surprised.

"Yeah, Mom," they plainly replied.

Throughout the following week, I asked each one of them what the difference was. My highly intuitive child explained, "You're here more, Mom."

I do not have Facebook on my phone. I had never been on it 24/7, but as a stay-at-home parent, it made me feel connected to the adult world. What I didn't realize was how much it pulled me away from those I was with during the day. While it felt like I had connected with so many, the reality is I had connected with no one in a way that actually enriched a relationship. It took a conversation with my kids for me to see that reality.

Screens can help us live *a life shared*. Facetime is a gift to loved ones scattered around the country. Skype and Zoom allow me to work part-time from my Kentucky home for a company based in North Dakota. Screens are not bad or good, but how we use them matters. In the winter months, we watch Jeopardy multiple times a week as a family. We watch America's Funniest Videos almost every Sunday year-round. We enjoy these shows. We guess the answers and vote for our favorite videos. Both shows are a platform for conversation and family time. The shows are not more important than life. They are not a priority, but they draw us together.

These three questions can create opportunities to live a *life shared* through screens:

1) Why do we use screens? List each one you own and use.
2) How do they serve our needs? Remember it is a tool to help you.
3) How does our usage help strengthen relationship as a family? Tools should help rather than hinder.

The answers to these questions are endless and unique to every family. These questions offer guidance when we answer them honestly, remind us to value relationships with our kids over convenience, and invite us to use screens well.

Obstacle: Life Management

The management and demands of life can consume family conversations. As parents, we talk all the time. Life must be organized. Kids have schedules. We have our own schedules. The soccer practice was canceled. The birthday party still needs a birthday present. Errands must be run. A lot of texts, phone calls, and discussions make it happen. These are indeed important conversations because life must be organized, turning the daily grind into scheduled events. The obstacle is that calendar talk and family logistics can feel like *a life shared*. Those conversations are *life management* rather than a *relational dynamic* that shapes our families. Life management is a critical part of family life. It cannot be dismissed, or everything becomes utter chaos. This is not an obstacle we can discard from our life, but we can make it an opportunity for meaningful connection.

Opportunity: Life Shared

With five kids, I spend a lot of time driving. Car lanes, martial arts, wrestling, the grocery store, the library, play dates, youth group, and Sunday worship are weekly commitments. Whenever I can, I limit the number of kids in the car. I mute my phone, turn off the radio, and focus on the kid beside me. I ask questions about his favorite video game, the current book he's reading, his last play date, or an upcoming event of interest to him. Often, I must ask about a few different things. Sometimes they are not interested in meaningful connection. Other times we share and connect.

Mealtime provides connections for the whole family. For us, that meal is dinner. I know a family that connects over breakfast. Work and activities can impose on family meals, but most can find at least one or two times a week to gather together. The table provides a common space for the family to connect. Our oldest no longer lingers but eats and asks to be excused. My wise husband expects us all to be seated together for at least ten minutes. That moment gives us an opportunity to connect. Each kid may not engage in conversation, but we are together to listen and share. With years of this practice and so many kids, we never lack for conversation starters. With smaller families, that can be hard. With older kids, a new habit can be difficult to establish, but not impossible. Here are some ideas to implement:

- No phones at the table, especially yours.
- Model conversation. Ask questions. Listen. Respond.
- Let everyone have a chance to share.
- Invite the quiet one into the conversation.
- Limit the most talkative one.

Conversation, as a family dynamic, takes time to establish. Give it time. Be consistent. Day after day, what may appear to be insignificant can be the groundwork for meaningful conversation.

Obstacle: Not Enough Time Together

The older the kids get, the less time we spend together. The little ones beg for books to be read and play dough to be shaped. The older ones run here and there with their own adventures. The last time I had jury duty my kids rejoiced.

"We get a day with dad!" they cheered.

"Thanks, guys. You know how to make me feel loved," I playfully replied.

"No, Mom. You don't understand. We see you every day. Dad is at work and does projects on Saturdays. This is extra time," the oldest two explained.

Whether it is work schedules or busy household schedules, most of us wish we had more time together. Years ago, scientists said what mattered most was not quantity time, but quality time. Later they realized both quality and quantity time matter. It is hard to experience quality time when the quantity is limited.

Opportunity: It's A Date

The calendar can feel like our master, but it is a tool for our good. Schedule time together. I know, it's easier said than done. For years, my husband and I said we wanted to go on monthly dates. It took us thirteen years before we moved from the spoken desire to real practice. It has breathed life into our marriage and our family. The same is true for kids and parents.

The boys and I step away from the daily grind once a month. We go to lunch or out for ice cream. Once one kid had a fever, so we went to a drive-thru and came back home with burgers and fries. Our "mom-boy dates" give us something to look forward to. We plan our next outing or remember dates from the past. Each one of us values the time. It is a real practical way we live *a life shared.*

My husband does something different with them. He takes one or two at a time. It is not a monthly commitment, but it is a regular practice he keeps—hunting, driving around, fishing, or a trip to Cabela's. They each know they will get their turn. Once the last kid has had his turn, they start planning the next round of time with dad.

Along with our mom-boy dates and time with dad, we have our monthly family date. The first weekend of the month we go out to eat. We pick the restaurant, and the kids try to guess our destination. It's part of the fun. We sit far away from mounted TVs and spend time together with no phones and no friends. It is a time we set apart as family. I know several families that do a game night. Find what suits your family best, and schedule it. Just like mealtime, be patient. The routine will be established, and the connection will happen. You can live *a life shared* while you manage life.

Conversation Challenges

1. The quiet kid

What do you do with a quiet kid or a kid who answers questions with one-word replies? I have one like that. He is introverted. Sometimes he wants to be with me when I run errands, just the two of us. I take him with me, and he brings a book. He reads. I drive. We barely talk. He does not need a lot of conversation to feel connected, so I must ask smart questions.

"How was your day?" gets us no further than "Fine."

I have had to learn how to ask questions that draw him out. A pointed question about a book he is reading or his last adventure with a friend might yield two minutes of conversation instead of two seconds. When my quiet kid starts a conversation, I give myself to that moment as much as possible.

Another mom uses a journal to talk with her quieter child. A quiet kid will share life. You do not need to make her talk more. Learn how she expresses herself, what interests her, and meet her where she is in life. Quiet kids share life too—just differently than others.

2. Lack of common interests

Maybe this is not a problem for you, but it certainly is for me. My boys can talk all day with my husband about hunting and fishing. If it is not deer hunting, then it is ice fishing or turkey hunting. All year-round, there is an outdoor interest that carries the conversation between them. They share with each other. They learn from each other.

I do not hunt or fish. I have no interests in Legos® or propellants. I do not care for boy humor. I do not push the bounds of safety at every turn. I read books. I cook. I visit with friends. It can be hard for us to start up a conversation with our limited common interests, but we have one common interest that remains. We are interested in each other. They are interested in me. They love that I write. They love the food I cook…usually! We sometimes read the same book and talk about it with each other. Mostly we ask about one another's interests and listen while each other talks. We learn about each other this way. It seems so simple, and it is.

Recently I traveled for work with my oldest. He read most of the drive time. Out of nowhere, he asked me, "What do you want to do when we don't live at home anymore?"

I was surprised and delighted.

"I want to write, travel…"

"Of course, you'll come see us. What do you want to do without us?" he interrupted.

"I will come see you boys, but I love to travel, too. I want to go places I haven't been, and I want to share our home with lots of guests, have friends over for dinner, and invite people over who need a place to stay," I replied.

"That sounds about right," he nodded.

Like anything new, conversations can feel awkward at first. It can almost feel like an interview or first date when you are trying to get to know someone, but try it. You might like it.

3. You don't care

This is a hard truth. Sometimes I don't care about the conversation my kids want to have.

"Mom, can I show you the Nerf® Modulus gun I designed?"

"Mom, want to look at shotguns with me? I think I know which one I want."

I really don't care about any of this. I have tried. I don't want to listen to them talk on and on about something they are so into today, only to have no interest in it next month. Sometimes I do choose to listen. I make it an incentive.

"After you get your chores done, come show me your Nerf® Modulus design?"

Because I have five kids and I want to be fully present with each one, I limit my time. I set a timer for 10 minutes to listen to my kid's great fascination for the moment. If I don't set the timer, I will think two minutes has been a lifetime, and skip out on them. Before we start talking, I let him know that I only have ten minutes. For that time, that child has my full attention on his interest. I listen, and we connect as he shares, and I respond—

44

not because I care about Nerf® guns, but because I care about him. What is insignificant to me is important to him. When our kids invite us to share life, we need to take the opportunity. Welcome the invitation to build the relationship. Listen. Time is short. Send the message you care. Grab the timer and set it, if you have to.

When challenges discourage us, look for opportunities that await us. When we see obstacles and challenges, ask God to lead us to opportunities that empower us to live *a life shared* with our kids in the midst of them.

Jesus, help us overcome obstacles and challenges.
Show us how to make them
opportunities for conversations.

Your Turn To Share

Did you try something from chapter one "Give It A Try"? How did it go? What did you learn?

I have mom-boy dates. My husband goes on father-son outings. We also have family time. We try to balance the quantity of time with our kids to create space for quality time. What are things you have done with your kids to create quality time? What are things you could do to create quality time?

Screens, life management, too little time together, and challenges make conversation difficult to practice. Would you agree or disagree with these? Can you think of other obstacles or challenges that interfere with a conversation?

Can you remember a time when someone told you they were listening, but you knew they were not? How did that feel? What effect did that have on your relationship?

I listed two messages we can send to our children when they reach out to us.
"I am not available; I will pretend to listen, but hear nothing."
"I am available to listen and respond, even if it takes a moment."
How do you send each of these messages to your kids?

Give It A Try!

RESPOND. This week respond to your kids the first time they interrupt you. Look them in the eye at eye level. (It may seem silly, but it helps them know they are heard and seen.) Explain your need to finish your task before you answer them. Respond as soon as you finish your task, and be encouraging as you both learn this new relational skill.

THINK AND DISCUSS. Answer these questions as a family. Think through how screens can help you share life. What screens do we use? Why do we have them? How do they serve our needs and help us share life with one another? What boundaries do we need to set to make sure screens are a tool to help us, not hurt us as a family?

CREATE SPACE. In my family, we create opportunities for conversation. No phones or screens are allowed at the table. Model conversation— ask questions, listen, respond. Let everyone have a chance to share. Invite the quiet one into the conversation. Limit the most talkative one. Take time as a family to write down ways you can create space for conversation. You might even post a list of things to talk about when you gather together.

SCHEDULE A DATE. Dream together about things you want to do as a family and one-on-one. Plan some dates with your kids. Put them on the calendar and enjoy the anticipation before the date and the memories made.

BRAINSTORM. If you have a quiet child, brainstorm ways to have *meaningful conversations* with them. What might they enjoy talking about? Would something like a journal or blog be a good platform to use to share life with them? What quiet activities can you do together to create availability for when conversations may come?

BE HONEST AND LISTEN. When your kids talk about something you don't care about, be honest with yourself and accept that you aren't interested. Focus on how they feel about their interest. Listen to the details to ask questions. Listen for what interest your kid in the topic and connect over their delight.

Chapter Three

Conversation Boundaries

Conversation has boundaries defined by relationship and time. We talk with different people about different things. A conversation you have with a friend is different than a conversation you have with your kids. Cell phones make us constantly available, but they have a silent mode for a reason. No one is available 24/7 without negative consequences. The same is true in family relationships. While this makes sense, the busyness of life can make it difficult to think about and establish conversation boundaries. We talk when we can, and get frustrated when our kids impose and interrupt. Conversation boundaries help us create categories and limits for conversation.

Conversation Categories

1. Family Conversation Only (FCO)

When our oldest were nine and seven-years-old, we decided to share our family budget with the kids. It was a spontaneous decision with the motive to show the importance of multiple digit addition.

"We have a set amount of money each month—our

income. What do we have to use it for?"

Quickly, they named some expenses. Groceries. Our house. Gas. Tithe. Phone. Lights. Water. Mom-boy dates. They were surprisingly thorough. We rounded out the list and told them to total up the sum. As they added the numbers, I questioned myself. What did we just do? Our nine- and seven-year-old know how much money we make! The boys proudly announced the total sum. We were just under-budget. As the conversation ended, we explained,

"Boys, what just happened here is an FCO—family conversation only. We don't tell people how much money we make. It's just not something we need to talk about outside our family."

"We know, Mom," they replied with a deep understanding.

While they did the math, I thought maybe we had made a huge a mistake. Instead, we had our first FCO. As parents, we felt a bit insecure with the conversation. The kids felt included and trusted.

FCOs include anything you want or need to address with your kids, but do not want them to share outside of the home. Anything the kids are affected by, or need to be equipped to handle, can be an FCO. What it means to be male and female in the image of God is an FCO. When we need to change our spending habits, we have an FCO. After we announced a new pregnancy and a few weeks later a miscarriage, we had an FCO. The news about my dad's cancer was an FCO until I was ready to share with others. We attended the same church for seven years. As husband and wife, we discerned for two years whether to attend a new church. Once we decided, the long ACO (adult conversation only) became an FCO. We told the kids about the upcoming change. We answered questions, wiped tears, cried with them, and walked through the change together by faith. FCOs help us connect as a family, strengthen the relational dynamic of conversation, and allow us to live *a life shared.*

2. Adult Conversation Only (ACO)

FCOs began with ACOs—adult conversation only. One night at dinner, my husband started a conversation. It felt inappropriate for the kids, so I interrupted,

"I think this is an adult conversation only."

He nodded, and we spoke later. Another time, I started a conversation at dinner, which my husband interrupted,

"That's an ACO, dear."

"What is an ACO?" I asked.

"Adult conversation only," he winked and smiled.

ACO is now a common code in our family. Those conversations wait until the kids are in bed or we can lock ourselves in the bathroom with the fan on. ACOs are decisions for the family, discipline concerns, private conversations, and any potential change to life as we know it. ACOs are anything the kids do not need to know about at that time, if ever, but we need to discuss.

3. Kid Conversations Only (KCO)

The kids added their own category of conversation called KCO—kid conversation only.

"What are you talking about?" I asked the oldest two, who were whispering in their room.

"KCO, Mom," they said.

"KCO?" I asked curiously.

"Kid conversation only," they explained. I smiled and politely excused myself.

These categories of ACOs, FCOs, and KCOs are helpful guides for a family in conversation. When anyone says, "ACO," "FCO," or "KCO," we all understand the boundaries of the discussion at hand. These three categories make space for meaningful conversation.

When We Aren't Available

Parenting is full of tensions. In the chapter titled, "Conversation Obstacles, Opportunities, and Challenges," the emphasis was on the importance of our availability to our kids. Our kids need to know our commitment to them. They also need to know the limits of the relationship. No one can always give of themselves and continue to love well. To love well, we must get away. We see this example in the life of Jesus. He got away for prayer, took naps during the storm, attempted to keep a low profile at times, and spent time with friends in life-giving fellowship. Jesus was not always available—so He *could* be available. The same goes for us. Here are some practices that limit availability so we can love well.

"Good night."

After bedtime, my husband and I do things we need to do and then spend time together. It is time for each other and ourselves. It is not a time for chitchat or discussing matters from the day with the kids. The infamous bedtime stalls do not stand.

"We never talked about…."

"You said we would…. today."

"I'm not tired. I just thought I'd hang out with you?"

The answer to the stalling is unequivocally "no." There are rare exceptions. There are times when we need to talk privately with one child. Some conversations are not FCOs, but one-on-

one conversations as parent and kid. Sometimes we have good news to share that is for just one child. Sometimes we need to address an ongoing pattern that needs to change. With several kids and work schedules, one-on-ones are hard to make happen. We will postpone bedtime for such conversations, but that is the exception. The rule is bedtime means good night. Whatever was not done can wait for the next day.

"This is not your conversation."

Not all conversations are private or restricted to a limited audience. Life management talk is constant. When kids hear something of interest, they inquire, "What are you talking about?" "This is not your conversation," I reply.

I say this countless times a day. In the middle of a conversation with my husband, one of the kids intrudes. My reply is, "This is not your conversation."

I ask a child a question, and another offers parental instruction. I explain, "This is not your conversation."

As a child, I had a horrible habit of interrupting conversations. Those closest to me know it remains a habit dying a slow death. When my interest is piqued by a comment or excitement is sparked by the subject matter, it is easy to chime in. Kids are no different. We must guide and teach them how conversation works. It is easy to grow weary doing good as parents. How many times must we repeat ourselves, right? For encouragement, I will repeat in my head, and sometimes out loud, "Repetition works. Repetition works. Repetition works."

The key is not to bark, but guide. Kids are curious. Some are even nosey. Few are ill-intended. The older they get, the worse this behavior becomes because they want to be included in the adult conversation. Our role is to guide our kids in the art of conversation. If we still practice the art of conversation, how much more must our children practice it? When they interrupt, we can simply explain, "This is not your conversation."

"Give me five minutes."

As a stay-at-home mom with five boys, the noise is nearly constant. There are moments when I need a moment of quiet. This is a real need that requires boundaries with our kids. No one can talk or listen all the time. We must have moments of quiet or at least one moment of quiet in a day. So, we have an hour of rest almost daily. It gives everyone space and silence. It is our reset button.

When my husband comes home, the little ones swarm him. At dinner, the older kids talk constantly. He needs a moment of quiet, too. Whether we stay home or work all day, there are moments when we need to step away in order to finish the day well.

"Give me five minutes" has become the code for this need.

The younger ones are still learning, but the rest of us know what it means—leave that parent alone for five minutes. Do not ask questions. Do not tell them anything. Just give that parent five minutes to re-group. When the timer goes off, we will start again.

The five minutes is not an escape, but a discipline. When you feel like you are going to lose it, take five minutes. When you start to ignore everything your kids say and retreat to a screen, step out of the room and take five minutes. Five minutes is not a lot of time. Kids can wait five minutes. It takes time for a family to learn this boundary and life-giving skill, but its messages are powerful.

I need a moment.
I choose self-control as a gift from God.
I want to love you well.

This boundary requires some explanation for it to be effective. A simple explanation that you need a moment will suffice. Briefly, tell them why. Limit yourself to five minutes. Ask an older child to care for a younger one, if necessary. Set the timer and walk away. When the timer goes off, come back out. Thank them for the moment, and start again.

"Not now."

"Not now" is a lesson I had to learn as a parent. My kids have never said those words to me when I asked them a question or attempted to strike up a conversation. However, on more than one occasion they have said, "I'm kinda' doing something, Mom."

They have even politely ignored me. I used to think this was rude of them. One day I finally understood what was really happening. I was interrupting them.

When I am in the mood to chat, and they are busy with something, I have learned to let them be. Sometimes it is not a good time to connect. If my kids are reading, I do not bother them with conversation. As parents, we have boundaries—times we are available, and times we are not. Kids have boundaries, too.

True conversation is an exchange between people that builds a relationship. This means conversation cannot happen on our timetable as parents, especially if our children are busy with their own activities. Both parent and kid must be available. Respect for their boundaries models respect for our boundaries. With this relational dynamic, they know that we do not thoughtlessly interrupt them. On occasion when we must interrupt them—because we need to leave or have a time-sensitive question—they give us their attention more readily.

Meaningful conversation requires boundaries to enrich relationships. Some conversations are for our family. Some are for adults. Others are for kids. When we provide conversation categories like FCOs, ACOs, and KCOs, it makes sense to kids. Sometimes they know the category before we do. Sometimes conversations require limits for both parents and kids. Once we establish the boundaries necessary to live *a life shared* with our kids, we can practice them and thrive in wonderful ways as family.

Jesus, help us practice boundaries in conversations and relationships that bring life to our family.

Your Turn To Share

What was something new this week or from chapter two "Give It A Try" section that you tried? What did you learn about yourself? How did your kids respond?

How do you think FCOs, ACOs, or KCOs could help your family have meaningful conversations? What are the ways you already do this in your family?

Boundaries can be either restrictive, or life-giving. How did you feel about boundaries before you read this chapter? How do you feel now?

When have you experienced boundaries that strengthened relationships? What made those boundaries life-giving?

Jesus took time for himself, so he could be available to others. I shared about *adult time only* and *five minute* breaks. How do you (or how could you) take time for yourself that helps you be present for your kids? What do you need to do to make this happen?

Give It A Try!

OBSERVE. Look for boundaries you already have as a family. We have rules about bedtime that we stick to with few exceptions. Other families let kids talk as long as they want at bedtime. Consider how your boundaries allow you to share life. Keep doing what works. Consider changes you might want to make.

CONVERSE. Introduce FCOs, ACOs, and KCOs to your family. Together talk about what conversations fit in these categories for your family.

- Do you have any ACOs that could include children so they can provide input or learn from your modeling?
- Do you have any FCOs that need to become ACOs for a while?

STUDY. Read Scripture and look for times when Jesus was alone to pray and rest. What was going on around Him in these moments?

IT'S A DATE! Schedule time for yourself to do something you enjoy—coffee with a friend, exercise, a hobby you once enjoyed. Reflect on how you interact with your family after your time away. Work toward the goal of regularly doing this. It is a discipline that will bring life to your family.

❧

Chapter Four

Conversation with Kids

Kids are a constant moving target. Just as soon as you figure out how to parent them, the rules change. The clingy little one becomes independent, only to become clingy again. Your first grader seems unable to hold instruction but can memorize every song she loves. Our tweens move from agreeable to moody. One thing holds fast. Meaningful conversation with our kids can happen when we let kids be kids.

Kids are kids, not adults. This may seem obvious, but it is easy to forget. Kids do not think like adults. They do not converse like adults. They do not ask questions like adults. Our older kids want us to listen to them but are not likely to listen to us as well. When they get going, they talk on and on, and suddenly lose interest when we share for any length. The practice of conversation, as a true exchange, takes time. When we let kids be kids, we do not expect our older ones to listen to us as well as we listen to them. Instead, we let them practice sharing while we model listening and responding as part of conversation.

The Stories They Tell

Our young ones tell wild stories as if they are a reality. My three-year-old tells stories of hunting, fishing, and cutting down trees. He kills deer, catches big fish, drives the truck, and even uses the chainsaw. He rattles on like a true storyteller. We listen and try not to laugh.

"Really? You drove the truck and shot a big deer?" I ask.

"Yeah, when I was eighteen," he answers.

"Wow. I bet that was so exciting!" I play along.

"Yeah," he concludes his grand adventure.

I would not have played along as well with my first few kids. The story is nonsense. None of it is true, but I have learned to let my kids be kids. His older brothers were taught how to play the game—to listen to his dreams that he shares as reality. He is not lying. He is a kid, who feels like a part of our family, as he shares in the adventures of our big boys through conversation.

Older kids, who talk more than they listen, and younger kids, who tell wild tales, are not exceptions, but the norm. Kids can be imaginative and playful one moment, and shift to being literal and serious the next. They ask questions daily and often without context. They make sudden significant statements that catch you off guard. And, they can jump from one conversation to the next without warning. From age two to twelve, they are busy making sense of the world around them and the world within. There is so much information and understanding they still need. We know this, yet amidst our daily life, we forget this and feel frustrated when kids act like kids.

A friend of mine had a kid who told quite the series of stories when he was in second grade. They were fact-based and believable, but not likely. She wasn't sure what to make of his accounts. One day after he told his latest tale, she simply asked,

"Did this really happen or is this something that could happen?"

"It could happen," he replied with a clever smile. That was usually his reply. He was not lying. He was telling a story of what could be. He was processing new information, enjoying his imagination, and delighting in his newly developed skill of storytelling. He got to do all of that because his mother let him be a kid. As an employee in our local elementary school, this experience with her son has served her well, again and again, with her students. She lets them be kids, as they share life with her.

Words that Don't Make Sense

Sometimes we simply don't understand what our kids are saying. I misunderstand our three-year-old on a daily basis. At some point, we play the guessing game until I get it right. Countless times my older kids have added a new word to their vocabulary, but mispronunciation makes it hard to recognize. I still don't remember how one kid said "vicinity," but I remember I kept saying, "I'm sorry. Can you say that again?" until I caught on.

"V-i-c-i-n-i-t-y?" I spelled out for clarification.

"Yeah," he replied.

"It's *vu-sin-i-tee*," I explained.

"Really?" he replied.

"Really. No one will know what you are talking about otherwise. It's *vu-sin-i-tee*," I assured him.

Some kids misspeak for various reasons. It is a symptom of dyslexia. To this day, one of my kids still says "aminal" instead of "animal." The worst ever was when he said "vulva" when he meant "Volvo." Because I knew him, I knew what he meant and why he made the error. "It's not vul-va. It's Vol-vo,"

I gently corrected. "Oh yeah, Volvo," he said. Some of our kids giggled. We all smiled and moved along with our discussion about cars. That could have been an awful moment. Instead, it was a teaching moment because we could let them be kids who sometimes mix up words, and giggle at innocent mistakes.

Kids also use words that mean different things to adults. Every generation, kids come up with new ways of using words. When my oldest started saying, "That's sick!" I had no idea what he was talking about. I had to ask. *Sick* means *cool* these days. My youngest at three-and-a-half insists that half-and-half is coffee-milk. Half-and-half means nothing to him, but coffee-milk makes sense because it is the milk I put in my coffee every day. Words that make sense are always the goal in our conversation, so for him it is coffee-milk. That works for us until one of the older kids comes in and insists it is half-and-half and the little one yells, "No it not. It coffee-milk!" Once again I remind the older kids, "It's okay if he calls it coffee-milk. He's three. Let him be three."

Let Kids be Kids

When people ask me the hardest part of mothering five boys, my answer is always the same, "Letting each one be who they are and where they are in life." A twelve-year-old is twelve. My eleven-year-old is eleven. That may seem silly, but when I am with the three-year-old and turn on a dime to be with the nine-year-old, I must shift gears to let each kid be who they are. Sometimes, I literally must look at a child and tell myself, "He's nine, Ellen. Nine. Not three. Not twelve. Nine." Then they grow up and I must learn all over again how to let them be who they *are*, instead of who they *were*. There have been nights when my husband walks by and whispers, "Remember, he's only five."

Other times I remind him. Life carries us away. We want things to move along faster and be easier. We forget as we shift from one kid to the next, to let each kid be the kid they are.

Kids forget to let each other be kids, too. Our older kids get easily irritated with our younger kids because they are not like them—like the coffee-milk vs. half-and-half debate between my eleven-year-old and three-year-old.

"Remember he's only three," I explain as an older child grumbles about coffee-milk being half-and-half. "You were three once, and we let you be three," I gently remind him. In that moment, I let both kids be the kids they are—one who uses words that make sense to him, and one who is frustrated with a little kid.

When we let kids be who they are, and meet them where they are in life, we can share life with them in ways that bring each of us great joy. We can live a life shared through meaningful conversation. This does not just happen. It is a choice we make again and again. Our awareness that kids are kids, and the intentional choice to honor them as kids, can be expressed in three areas—attention, patience, and laughter.

Attention.

We all need to be seen and heard by those we love. Kids need to know we see them and hear them. We meet these needs when we give them our attention. For kids, attention is not when we pretend to listen as we finish an email or phone call. Attention is when we stop, set down the task at hand, and look our kids in the eye, which communicates we're available to listen and respond. Attention is not easy to give. It is a choice we make. It is an expression of love, an act of honor. In the moments we give our kids undivided attention, we give them more than we can ever imagine. We give them ourselves. We build on the foundation of our relationship. Even more, we give them a sense of worth as one seen and heard. But who has time for undivided attention? It can feel impossible in our society that values busyness, multi-tasking, and efficiency.

A thirteen-year-old daughter shared with me how sometimes she just needs her mother to give her undivided attention. No phone calls. No sibling interruptions. No chores or work. Just her attention. The mother confessed the difficulty she has with this. I suggested maybe the daughter could communicate her need for undivided attention with a code word. Now when she walks into the kitchen and ask to talk, and it's not a good time for her mother, she can reply, "Later?" The mom knows that means, "Okay, but I need to talk with you. I need your undivided attention." The mom had no idea how she would ever learn to follow-up with her daughter. The answer was to put it on her calendar before bed that day. The mom could answer her daughter, "Yes, tonight before bed."

With younger kids, it is different. Maybe you play a game together. Perhaps you listen to their stories or answer their questions on a walk, or read the pile of books they love while you cuddle. Little kids do not have long attention spans. When my younger kids need my attention and interrupt me for it, I have developed a consistent reply, "I want to hear what you have to say. I can't right now. One moment and I will be able to listen." With repetition, they learn to wait a moment for my undivided attention. I listen, respond, and off they go again.

At various times, we all give our kids attention. When they need our attention, and we do not want to give it, we must exercise patience toward them.

Patience.

There are days when patience seems like it's a gift given in vain. One day I found myself defeated within. The patience I offered seemed worthless and lost. What good was coming from it? As I sat with one son, weary from the weeks, months, and years of patience over the same thing, I asked the Lord, "What does this look like to you? Is patience really the gift he needs right now?" I thought maybe it was an *enough is enough* moment, time for me to take a hands-off approach instead of a gentle presence, and move on. Suddenly, I could see us seated there from outside myself. My son was nestled in my arms with a book he labored to read, and huge, healthy fruit surrounded us. It was beautiful. "Thank you, Lord," I prayed silently. "Thank you." I took a deep breath, and sat patiently with my son. I was grateful I sought the Lord and He answered me.

After a hard moment with one kid, I have told the others, "One of your brothers just used up most of my patience. There's not much left for you. Seriously." It became a routine announcement. And then God spoke to my heart, *Really? Is that how my patience works? Patience is from me. You are not patient. I give my patience to you, and my patience never runs out. You have the patience to give if you will give it."* This is a revelation I continue to live into. I can always give my kids patience if I am willing to cry out for it, and choose love for them rather than weariness because of them.

When the questions are endless, when we are interrupted countless times, when one kid has a really bad day, when the one who is the hardest for us to love pushes every single button, and when we can't hear ourselves think—bedtime doesn't come soon enough. In those moments, we can have patience when we ask for it. This is not my privilege; this is our privilege. This is what it looks like to love our kids sacrificially, to let the strength of Christ be ours in our weakness. Patience is a gift from Him to receive and share. When we accept it and offer it to our kids as an act of love, we can let kids be kids; and we can live *a life shared* through conversation.

Laughter.

Sometimes you just have to laugh. The younger one tells fantastical tales, and you laugh together. The independent kid spills milk on the table, and it runs all over the floor. You can cry, scream, or sigh. It took me a long time, but I find it far better to laugh and grab a rag. Kids are silly and messy. They stumble forward as they learn new skills by dropping things, putting shoes on the wrong feet, and using words that make no sense. Laughter goes a long way. It helps us connect in awkward or upsetting moments. Laughter turns hearts towards love and turns little things that could upset us, into a moment we share with one another. It helps us enjoy our kids being kids.

When the older one tells you how you hold her back from her potential, you listen while you laugh inside. She thinks she is ready for the world. However, she is still learning to take care of herself and her own room. Your son announces he completed his chore, but evidence suggest otherwise. You laugh inside as you remember when you were a kid, your father sounded just like you will sound when you walk through what a "job well done" looks like regarding the chore.

Life is hard. Parenting is hard. Some days it is extremely tough. Laughter stirs delight in our hearts, restores perspective, and reminds us that kids are kids. One day they will be adults; but today, they are kids.

Kids are Kids

Kids are not adults. Wild stories to process life, words that don't make sense, and the different development stages can leave a parent confused. One day your five-year-old counts at random, only to master counting overnight. Your eight-year-old insists on more independence because she knows she is ready for it, but you resist because in your mind she only has the skill set of a seven-year-old. Kids change and the older they get, the greater the changes. With the demands of family life and adulthood, it can be challenging to let our kids be kids. However, the rewards are tremendous when we let them be who they are and where they are in life. When we listen carefully, give them our attention, offer the patience of our good God, and welcome the gift of laughter, we can know our kids and share life with them through meaningful conversation.

Jesus, help me let my kids be who they
are and where they are in life.
Help me give them my attention, your patience,
and laughter so we can share life together.

Your Turn To Share

My three-year-old can tell quite a story! What are some stories your kids have told or some of their funny word mix-ups?

What are some of your favorite memories of your kids being kids? What are some of your favorite memories of when you were a kid being a kid?

What can be difficult about listening to your kids—not just slowing down to hear or decipher their words—but really listening to their hearts? What is difficult about taking the time to respond to them, letting them know that you understand their heart?

I must remind myself the ages of my kids, so I maintain realistic expectations of them. What helps remind you to let your kids be where they are in life?

Attention, patience, and laughter help us let kids be kids. How have these gifts helped you share life with your kids and create space for conversation?

As a parent, what would it look like to give, not from yourself, but from all that God has given you?

Give It A Try!

REMEMBER. Think back to when you were a kid. Remember what it was like for you to be the same age as your kids.

GIVE YOUR ATTENTION. When your kids pursue you, give them yourself. You may need to schedule it or allow the moment to happen even if it feels like an interruption. Focus on being with your kids at that moment—listening, hearing, and responding to them.

LAUGH. Choose laughter and enjoy your kids being kids. Notice your response to the crazy stories and the misspoken words. Choose not to lecture or fuss, but see the moment from the eyes of your kids. Ask God to help you laugh and enjoy your kids as kids.

SEEK PERSPECTIVE. Sometimes we need to know we are not the only ones. Talk with friends about things their kids do and ask how they respond. Talk about your own childhood and how your parents responded or reacted to you. Community can help turn daily woes into normal family life.

PRAY. I rarely pray alone and uninterrupted anymore, but I pray all the time. I pray for strength, guidance, patience, peace, forgiveness, and so much more as a parent. Ask God to give you what you need to parent your kids. Don't be afraid to pray out loud in the moment of need. It is good for our kids to witness our need and reliance on God. Let Him care for you, support you, and love you so that you may do the same for your kids.

Chapter Five

———— 🙢 ————

Hard Conversations

Some of you skipped ahead to this chapter. A friend apologetically explained that this is the only chapter she has interest in. Everyone knows they need help with the hard conversations, and I do hope to write a book about hard conversations one day. This book is about the role of conversation to strengthen family relationships. Not every conversation is meaningful, but *every* hard conversation has the potential to be meaningful.

A hard conversation is hard because you know you need to talk about a certain subject, but you don't want to, or don't know how to. Often it is personal—family conflict, illness, loss, confession and forgiveness, substance abuse, adoption, foster care. You have your own feelings and thoughts. Hard conversations are awkward by nature, and too often we lack examples to show us the way. The unknowns that surround hard conversations are many. What do I say? What if they ask a question I can't answer? How much information is too much information? When is the right time?

Hard conversations often surprise us, and we find

ourselves feeling backed into a corner where the only way out is through the conversation. Some have written *scripts* for hard conversations. Life is not a play, however, and we are not characters in a movie. Life is real. This chapter offers examples, encouragement, and tools to help us all face hard conversations that life presents.

Kids ask questions.

In our society, you address questions with answers, but what if you don't have to have the answer? It happens to me all the time. As parents, we are asked countless questions. Sometimes kids ask questions we don't know how to answer. We could easily dismiss or Google these questions. However, the great thing about questions without answers is they can lead to conversation. Below are two great responses that encourage conversation from questions without answers.

"That's a good question. I don't know. Why do you ask?"

"I don't know. What interests you in _____?"

A question in response to a question can lead to the context we often lack with younger children. When they ask a question without any reference, our questions fill in the gaps. Sometimes I ask more questions than offer answers in a conversation with young kids. A question in response to a question invites older kids to express themselves and ask better questions. Remember kids are always learning, so the question is not so much about an answer as it is about processing their world and understanding all the information they already possess.

"Does space ever run out?" my six-year-old asked from the backseat.

"What do you mean?" I replied.

"Well, when they are in space do they ever run into walls?" he asked.

"No, they have never run into walls while in space," I answered.

"That's what I thought," he explained decidedly.

It was short and sweet—a little moment when he asked a question as he pondered a mystery of the world. I simply listened, asked a question, and welcomed his wonder.

Kids of all ages ask lots of questions like the one above. They know a little bit about something, and it causes them to wonder about what they don't know. Some questions require more than a question. For those questions, I have four tools that help me share life with my kids.

Four Tools For Any Hard Conversation

These tools have aided our family through countless conversations. We've walked through cancer, infant and child loss with friends, extended family conflict, moves, unmet expectations, understanding the roles of everyone in blended families, marital strife, parental failure moments, miscarriages, sexuality as male and female, politics, and more.

1. Be Honest.

Honesty is the best policy. The idea of being honest with children never made sense to me, until I had children. Our kids always discover *convenient truths* and these must be addressed later. In the end, they are not true, nor are they convenient. With children, honesty is black and white. From their perspective, you either lied or you told the truth. It becomes easy for kids to tell convenient truths themselves as they grow older. However, they expect more from us—and rightly so.

Honesty strengthens relationships. Kids are trusted in moments of honesty, and they know it. When we are honest with our children, they learn two significant lessons:

1) They can be honest with us.
2) They can put their trust in us as their parents.

So often parents assume their kids will trust them, but trust must always be earned and proven worthy of investment. Why? Because honesty requires courage, and courage always comes with risk. Honesty is always the best policy.

At five-years-old, a child asked questions to understand the relationships in our extended family. My parents divorced when I was eight-years-old, and both remarried later in life. When the five-year-old was told that my mother and father were once married, he shook his head and said, "Now I'm really confused." All he has ever known is Grandma and Sandman, Pappaw and SherSher.

"I know. It is confusing," I assured him.

The older kids nodded, "Yep, but it's true."

Painting pretty pictures of our families would be easy. A FCO can help a child understand why she has six grandparents while her friend has only four. Families with secrets discourage honesty and openness because some are *in the know* and some are not. No child needs to know every family dynamic, but when they ask a question or someone brings it up, be honest in your answer. Honesty is always the best policy.

2. Keep it simple.

Simply answer the questions they ask. As parents, we feel sometimes obliged to make every moment a teaching moment. We quickly over answer and over explain. Remember, kids are kids. They will ask you twenty questions to get the answer they need, but they only want you to respond to the question they asked. If you don't understand the question, ask questions until you do. When the conversation begins with you, simple means brief. We call it the *Readers Digest* version. If they need more information, they will ask more questions.

"Boys are boys and girls and girls, right?" one of the boys repeatedly asked when he was four.

"That's right," we told him.

It can feel more difficult with older kids. One of the boys received a special invitation to participate in an extra-curricular activity. The activity came with a time commitment and financial investment. I was so happy for him, but I knew it was not an option due to the expense.

"Mom, what do you think? Can I do this?" he asked as we drove home.

Everything in me felt obliged to explain why he could not participate because of the expense, our budget, and previous financial commitments. He knew about our monthly expenses and income from a previous FCO. I was ready to launch my case with much regret. Instead, I asked him a question, "Well, if you did that, what would we have to stop doing?"

"What do you mean?" he asked.

"Well, we spend our money on certain things. What would we not do for you to do this?"

He thought through some options. Each one he ruled out on his own.

"I think it's best if I don't do this," he decided.

My heart was heavy, but so proud. He figured it out for himself. You can only do what you can afford. We could afford it, but only if we stopped doing something else for our family.

He had come to a decision himself because I kept things simple and honest. We had the money. We had simply chosen to use it in other ways.

"I'm going to pray for God to provide a way for you to do this," I concluded.

Later that year, he was invited to join the extra-curricular activity again. This time the invitation included a scholarship. The meaningful conversation from months ago, which led us to pray for God's provision, made us both smile.

3. Use terms that make sense to them.

When you have an answer but don't know how to talk about it on a level that the child can understand, what do you do? Think about it from their perspective. Years ago, one of the kids asked me why I killed Jesus. He was only four-years-old. I had no idea what to say. Two seminary degrees had not equipped me for that moment.

"That's a big question. Let me think about it," I replied to buy time.

I thought for a moment. What would make sense to my sweet four-year-old? What can he understand?

"I wanted my way more than anything else," I explained.

He sat there silently processing my answer. We had talked a lot about how he could not always do things the way he wanted. Even mommy and daddy couldn't always do things the way we wanted to. He understood *wanting his way more than anything else*. He asked more questions, pressing me and my guiltiness. I simply agreed and repeated my answer, "I wanted my way more than anything else." What could have been avoidance on my part, or a theological monologue, became a meaningful conversation because I answered his question in a way that made sense to him. The whole moment was a precious gift from God.

There are all sorts of things we say to our kids, and they say to each other. Here are some examples.

Why can't we watch that movie? *"Different families, different rules."*

When friends and family have died: *"God didn't want this for us. He made us for life."*

When the kids condemn another: *"Sometimes we make bad choices, too."*

When people are labeled good or bad: *"We are all bad guys without Jesus. He makes us good."*

When the kids mistreat each other: *"Jesus said, treat your brother the way you want to be treated."*

4. Present the facts.

When our oldest was six, we had a miscarriage. We had told the kids, family, and friends we were pregnant. A week later the pregnancy was at risk. I spent a long weekend on the sofa and in bed. The pregnancy ended in a miscarriage. We told our boys we weren't going to have our baby because our baby had stopped growing.

"Why?" our oldest asked, confused.

"I don't know," I honestly replied

"Our baby is dead?" he questioned.

"Yes," I explained.

"Where is our baby?" he asked.

"You know how every month my body makes a home for a baby just in case a baby needs one? Well, that home wrapped up our baby, and our baby slid right out of my body. I couldn't see our baby because our baby was so very tiny," I answered gently.

"Our baby is just gone?" he asked.

"Our baby is not with us. Our baby is with Jesus," I concluded.

Less than two months later, I was pregnant again. For some crazy reason, I kept the pregnancy test. Every so often our seven-year-old would get the pregnancy test, which still read positive. He would hold it and announce confidently, "Still pregnant!"

I realized he was concerned about another miscarriage. He never said that, but that was why he repeatedly checked the pregnancy test and asked lots of questions during that pregnancy.

"Where is our baby? I know he is not in your tummy. People say that, but there is acid in there. That would hurt our baby. Where is he?" my seven-year-old asked out of nowhere.

"You are right. He is not in my tummy. Are you ready for a new word? He is in my uterus. It is a special place God made just for our baby to grow until he is ready to be with us in our arms," I explained.

"I knew he wasn't in your tummy," he replied.

When I answered his questions and he checked the pregnancy test, he was comforted and assured that our baby— this baby—was well.

Questions That Require More Than One Tool

With these tools and conversation as a relational dynamic in our families, we stand ready for the hard conversations life will afford. A little practice does go a long way. Some conversations require a combination of the tools, and maybe all four tools.

When one of the boys was five, he announced that his penis sometimes bounced over hills as we drove down the road. He concluded, "And sometimes it just stands straight up!" My five-year-old marveled at the workings of his body. The eight-year-old replied, "Yeah. Why do they do that?" I had a few choices. I could act like I didn't hear him, or tell him we would talk about that later in hopes he would forget, or answer his question.

"You know God gives husbands and wives the gift of sex. Well, the husband's penis must stand up. It must be erect to have sex," I replied and was glad we didn't have to look at each other as I drove down the road.

For years, we had modeled openness to their questions, so he asked a very specific question about something he had clearly pondered before. He felt a bit awkward. Despite the awkwardness, he took the risk because he knew our relationship was a safe space for such inquiry. I answered the question he asked. I was honest. I kept it simple. I used terms that made sense to him. I presented the facts—just the facts. These four tools made a hard conversation, not so hard. You can do this with your kids, too. It takes practice, but now you have the tools you need. Below is a helpful guide that will help you address the hard conversations.

- Embrace the awkward.
- Be honest.
- Keep it simple.
- Use terms that make sense to them.
- Present the facts, just the facts.
- Repeat for every hard conversation.

Hard conversations can bring life to our families and strengthen our relationships. They are worth the awkwardness and risk. The risk calls for courage, but the courage to be honest teaches our kids to be honest with us and invites them to trust us.

When we keep it simple, use terms that make sense to them, and present just the facts, we honor our kids. We meet them where they are and let them be who they are.

Hard conversations with our kids allow us to share all of life with our kids, and create opportunities for more meaningful conversation with our kids. Finally, hard conversations invite us to live by faith. Life is full of unknowns, loss of control, and circumstances no one wanted. When we name those things, when we admit our lack of knowing, when the answer is *no,* and we wish it were *yes*, we can reach out in faith to the One who sees, hears, and knows all. We can talk with Him and walk by faith with our kids. It would be easier for us to walk by sight, but for now, we must walk by faith through the hard conversations. When we walk together with our trust in the One who is faithful, the hard conversations can only enrich our shared lives.

Jesus, help us hear our kids and respond,
especially when the conversations are hard.

Your Turn To Share

Each week you are trying something from "Give It A Try" or an idea of your own. How did it go this week? Has anything surprised you?

Kids often ask questions to help process their world. When have your kids done this and were not interested in your answer? What do you think they were processing?

What is a hard conversation you had with your kids that went well? What made it go well?

Four tools help us have hard conversations. Be honest. Keep it simple. Use terms that make sense. Present the facts. How could these tools help you work through hard conversations?

What were hard conversations for your parents when you were a kid? What do you wish you could have talked to them about? How might it have impacted your life and relationship if they had done so?

How does the suggestion to *embrace the awkward* help you choose hard conversations with your kids?

Give It A Try!

LISTEN. When your kids ask questions, listen—not to answer, but understand why they are asking the question. Where is their curiosity coming from? What are their concerns? Respond with what you heard to cultivate the conversation. If you're wrong, your kid will tell you.

ASK A QUESTION. When your kids ask a question, respond by saying "That's a great question. What do you think?"

NAME AND IDENTIFY. Hard conversations are just hard. List conversations that are hard conversations for your family. Identify what makes them hard. Consider which tool could help you embrace each conversation.

ROLE PLAY. When you role play with another adult, it can help you feel more comfortable when you talk with your kids. It feels very silly and can't prepare you for everything, but it helps identify what is uncomfortable for you and helps you feel more prepared.

GET SUPPORT. You are not alone. Ask your pastor or a friend with older kids for resources and support. Share with a friend or family member you trust. People who understand or have kids the same age can provide much-needed support.

Chapter Six

Conversation Encouraged

Have you ever wondered if you encourage or discourage conversation with your kids? Have you ever wondered how they experience your role in the conversation? If you are reading this book, you want your kids to share their life with you. You want them to answer personal questions about their life, and you want them to come to you with their fears and uncertainties.

The market is filled with conversation starters. They can spark an exchange, yet they do not cultivate a *relationship* sustained by conversation. Parents can invite and encourage kids to share their day-to-day life with us. We also have the power to silence them. In fact, there are many ways we shut down conversation with our kids. Fortunately, there are many ways to cultivate conversation. How our kids experience our role in a conversation matters. We can encourage conversation when we make it part of our parent-child relationship. We can foster a relational dynamic with our kids that allows conversation to carry us through life.

"I wonder what they did today," I commented to the parent in the hallway as we waited for our preschool children.

"I ask every day, but my son never shares," she replied.

I spoke before I thought, "Really?"

"Really. I don't even know why I ask. Why? Does your son tell you?"

"Yes. Not necessarily when I ask, but when it comes to mind, he shares about a letter he learned or an art project they did. Usually, I get a snack report during lunch." It was awkward. She wanted this kind of conversation with her son.

Relationship Roles

Parent, not friend.

For parents to encourage conversation, our role needs to be clear to our kids. We are the parent. They are the kids. We all want to be the parents that our kids share their lives with, so we might confuse being their friend, with being their parent. The temptation is real. The idea of being *friends* with our kids is seen in families, as well as with teachers in schools.

When our firstborn attended kindergarten, everyone there was your *friend*. The teachers called the students *friends*, and the students called the teachers *friends*. However, they weren't *friends* because the teachers were in charge. They handled classroom management with a behavioral system to reward and condone behavior. The teachers controlled the schedule. The relationship between the teachers and students was one of hierarchy, not friendship.

When we relate to our children as friends, we send contrary messages regarding our role in the parent-child relationship. As parents, we correct our kids for their behavior. Often discipline is met with resistance and disappointment, or even anger, which is directed toward us. Even though parents understand this—and may even empathize with their child's feelings—they need to let the correction stand. This demonstrates love toward them. When parents change the rules trying to make the upset child happy again, the role of the parent as the caretaker is forfeited for the desire to be their friend. It is confusing for the child. When we choose to be the parent for the sake of our kids, our kids learn their role and ours. When we bounce between being the parent and the friend, it makes it hard for our kids to know who they're sharing with—the parent or the friend. This lack of clarity is a risk for kids—a risk most will not take. An eleven-year-old once explained to me, "The primary role of parents is to be there for us, not for us to be there for them. With friends, you help each other. It's just different with parents."

Parents care for kids. We feed them, clothe them, teach them, guide them, correct them, and love them. We are responsible for providing these things for them. Our kids are entrusted to us for their well-being in our family and community. Friends are not responsible for such care and growth. We share life with our friends. They are our safe places in life. Regrettably, friends come and go. Parents stay, or at least are supposed to. Parents can express to their kids through their actions and words, "I am for you, not against you. I hear you, and I see you. I am committed to care for you and protect you, even from yourself. You don't have to like me, but know I love you. I am the parent. You are the child. You are worth great sacrifice and love, and that is mine to give you. Your heart is safe with me." Parents can give so much more than a friend. I smiled when one eleven-year-old explained; "You can't love your friend like you love your mom."

This kind of parenting can establish the foundation for friendship in the adult child-parent relationship. But how do we do it? We repeatedly choose to encourage conversation through our actions and words. This will cultivate a healthy parent-child relationship. Let's look at some things we can do to encourage our kids to have conversations with their parents.

For them, not against them.

Kids know when we are *for* them. They just know. As parents, it is easy for our kids to think we are *against* them. We restrict them from things they want to do. We discipline them for things they did and did not do. I remind my older kids often, "I'm for you." They know it, but they also need to hear it. Sometimes, we unknowingly do things that suggest we are not for them, but against them. Once we realize this, we can take responsibility for our role in the relationship and make changes that encourage conversation. I remember when I looked at one of the boys and said with tears in my eyes, "I really am trying."

"I know, Mom. I know," he replied tenderly. He knew I was *for* him.

To be for them, and not against them, we must choose them again and again. We welcome one-on-one conversation. We talk with them, see them as people, talk kindly to them, ask sincere questions, and operate out of love. These things— individually and collectively—say to our kids, "I am for you, not against you. I hear you, and I see you. I am committed to care for you and protect you, even from yourself. You don't have to like me, but know I love you. I am the parent. You are the child. You are worth great sacrifice and love, and that is mine to give you. Your heart is safe with me."

Welcome one-on-one conversation.

Our kids need us to welcome them into relationship through conversation. We can welcome one-on-one conversation two ways—initiation and reception. We invite our child into relationship through conversation, and we embrace the conversation our child initiates.

"I had no idea how much we needed one-on-one conversation," a mother with older kids declared. "We have a lot of family conversation, but not as much one-on-one conversation. I see how much more intentional I must be."

A parent of two older kids, who has recently begun practicing conversation—a true exchange with her kids— shared a key to welcome conversation. "I am learning to re-visit conversations. Sometimes it takes three or four times of visiting the same conversation for them to share. I am also learning to ask questions, and give space and time for them to answer."

Another parent shared, "We have conversations in the crevices. Sometimes, though, I can hear in my daughter's voice when it's really important. Then we step into my bedroom and I listen. I want her to know she can come to me with anything."

These parents choose to welcome conversation with their kids. One of them realized the need for conversation and is figuring out how to make it happen, one has begun this practice, and one has always practiced conversation. We all like to think we initiate conversation with our kids and welcome the conversations they initiate. Our children's perspective is insightful.

"When I am talking to my mom," an older child admitted, "and my sister comes in and interrupts, and they never come back to me, I feel rejected. It's already hard for me to share. It makes it a lot more difficult."

"Have you ever told her that's how you feel and that you need her to encourage you to share?" I asked. He shook his head, *no*. The look on his face made it clear that such a conversation was not a risk he felt he could take.

Life is full of interruptions. Conversation can fall right through the cracks. We can miss their cues, and let life interrupt them. We can also choose to welcome and initiate conversation with our kids.

Talk with them, not at them.

I love to talk, but I love conversation more than the sound of my own voice. Parents talk to their kids. We do well when we talk *with* them and not *at* them. You know the difference. It's when someone talks a monologue but never makes space for you to share. There is no exchange. This is an easy pattern to fall into as a parent. We have things to do and places to go. Instructions must be given and followed. Loading my five kids into the car in a timely manner, without incident, is no small feat! Every single time we gather to leave the house, one of them attempts to start a conversation. "We're not talking right now. We're getting ready. Get your shoes on. We'll talk in the car," I explain. In the car, I follow up. "Okay, I'm ready to listen now."

Sometimes we need to talk *to* them. Other times, we must talk *with* them. Parents must do both to encourage conversation in the relationship. That is what we do when we listen and respond to them. For some, the response part is the hardest. You listen actively, but a verbal response does not naturally roll off the tongue. It is important to listen when our kids share with us, but they only know we heard them when we actively respond to them.

A meaningful conversation must be a true exchange, and that is only possible when we talk *with* our kids. This subtle difference transforms relational dynamics and the opportunity to share life with one another.

"It's not what you say, but how you say it."

"It's not what you say, but how you say it," was a mantra of my father's. If I heard it once, I heard it a thousand times as a teenager. Now as a parent, I know how true it is. Sometimes one of my kids will say something in a rude or sassy tone. It can be difficult to hear what they said because of how they said it. The same applies to us as parents.

"Are you listening to me?" my oldest barked at the five-year-old.

"Wow, do I talk to you that way?" I asked sincerely.

"Sometimes," he snapped back.

"I didn't know that. I don't want to talk to you that way, and I am not going to allow you to speak to your brother that way."

He sighed.

"Here's what's going to happen. Both you and I will stop talking that way," I concluded.

If we want to teach our kids that the way they speak to each other matters, we must listen to ourselves through our kids. They echo us. It's a good way to realize how we speak to them. When we ask our kids to speak to one another kindly, we must choose the same hard work for ourselves. We cause harm when we expect our kids to behave better than we do. When we set the example to listen to ourselves and change our tone, we encourage and empower meaningful conversation.

Questions, not accusations.

Sincere questions create space for meaningful conversation. Accusations create barriers in the parent-child relationship and silence conversation. My husband has helped me to learn this one. I would think I was asking a question, but I was assuming a behavior and often with fault. "What are you doing?" was not a sincere question, but a blaming accusation. Talk about a conversation stopper. I did it all the time. I still do sometimes.

I told my son to empty the dishwasher. A little while later I found him on the sofa reading and assumed he was procrastinating. "What are you doing?" I questioned with the implicit claim that he had not emptied the dishwasher. He responded with defense because he had already completed the task.

Slowly, I am learning to hear how I come across from my child's perspective. I choose to assume nothing and ask questions. "What are you doing?" I ask sincerely. I honor my son with respect in my tone and teach him that questions invite answers instead of passively state blame. Sometimes I get it wrong. I check myself. I acknowledge my wrong against him and try again. It's okay when we err. We all do. Our kids just need to know we want to get it right, and that we desire to honor them, not accuse them. Instead of making assumptions, we can learn to ask sincere questions to open conversation. Sincere questions assume nothing and welcome our kids into a safe relationship. Safe relationships encourage conversation.

See them as people.

"I love how you talk with kids like they are people." These words have been spoken to me on more than one occasion. "I know, right," I reply with a smile. Kids are not merely kids; they are people. We must let them think and feel what they think and feel, not what we want them to think and feel. During my interviews, a woman explained that she had never had a conversation with her parents. There was no true exchange. Declarations were made, and expectations were followed. To this day, there are no conversations with her parents—just confusion about why the adult kids aren't more like "the way we raised you to be."

On the television show, *Mr. Rogers' Neighborhood*, Mr. Rogers saw kids as people. He loved them. He looked at them. He gave time for them to respond when he asked questions. He treated kids like people. He did not belittle them or over-esteem them. He understood they had feelings, thoughts, and gifts to share with others. We are not Mr. Rogers. We are parents. But just like Mr. Rogers, we can choose to honor our kids as people. We can look them in the eye, give them time to respond in conversation, and treat them the way we want to be treated. This shift to seeing kids as people can transform the relational dynamic in our families.

Motivated by love.

"I need you to do what I said," I explained calmly, but wearily. It had been a rough morning. Everything inside of me wanted to yell at every little thing he did. My ten-year-old son replied sincerely, "So you don't get frustrated?"

I took a slow, deep breath and explained gently, "No, because I have given patience and gentleness to you all morning. I have chosen love over anger. It is good and right for us to love one another. We want to encourage each other to love, right?" He silently nodded. I smiled amazed at the words that poured from my mouth. I meant what I said. I wanted us to love each other in action, not just in word.

This is new for us. In the past, I got easily frustrated. I was not reliably patient or gentle. I could quickly become demanding. I would get upset. The kids would do what I said, and I would calm down. That was our pattern. I taught them to do what I said so that I wouldn't be frustrated. I knew it was not a good pattern. After reading *Scream Free Parenting* by Hal Edward Runkel, LMFT, I saw the pattern for what it was—emotional manipulation for my well-being. I began to beg God as my Father to break this destructive pattern and teach me one that was rooted in love. I did not want to curse our relationship with manipulation, but instead, bless our relationship with love. God had seen us and heard my cry.

We are instructed as parents to show our children the love of God, and to lead them into the way that brings life. We are not to exacerbate them but discipline them. God longs for us to live in this kind of relationship with our kids. More and more, I choose to parent out of His love. When I don't, I confess, repent, receive forgiveness from my child and Father in heaven, and rise again to love. Manipulation opposes safe life-giving relationships. There is no room for conversation. Love cultivates trusted, secure relationships filled with meaningful conversation.

It's Not About Getting It Right

Who do you share your life with—friends who constantly teach you things, correct all the little mistakes you make, tell you how to feel, turn down your invitations, do not follow up with you, call you by the wrong name, and treat you like less than a person? People who yell at you when they are upset and tired?

This is not who we long to be, but as parents, this is who we can very easily be toward our kids. I have been the momma who constantly corrects, and answers "I can't right now" to countless invitations. I rarely call them by their actual name, and forget to follow-up with them. The oldest child jokes I couldn't get their names right even if they wore name tags. I have monumental victories and epic-fails. How we relate to our kids is so very important, but we don't always get it right as parents.

One night I accidentally humiliated one of the kids. Afterward, I said, "Well that was probably my worst momma-moment." Three kids looked at me and announced in unison with much sarcasm, "Uh, no." "Oh," I stuttered in embarrassment. I was embarrassed, but grateful too. I'm grateful our relationship could weather my shortcomings and allow honest conversation about who we are and how we relate as a family.

Be encouraged. Parenting is not about always getting it right. Good parenting means we choose again and again to be the parent our kids want to share life with because conversation is encouraged in the relationship.

Jesus, fill us with Your love so we may
encourage conversation with our kids.

Your Turn To Share

As you think back over the past six weeks, how have you encouraged conversation with your kids? What is working? What is difficult for you?

How does our culture tempt you to be your kids' friend instead of their parent? How does this chapter help you define your unique role and privilege as the parent?

Do your kids talk with you about their days? Why do you think that is? How do you encourage them to share?

I offer seven ways we can encourage conversation with our kids. Which ones do you desire in peer relationships? Which way of encouragement do your kids need most from you?

Kids have thoughts and feelings just like we do. When are times your kids have shared their heart with you, and you empathized with them? When is that challenging—when you are in a hurry, don't agree with them, or are upset with them?

Apologies allow us to shift from getting it right to parenting out of love. How can apologies bring healing to your family and encouragement to you?

Give It A Try!

OBSERVE AND LISTEN. Try to figure out when your kids want to talk one-on-one with you. It may be in their posture, tone of voice, or sudden neediness. You might even say, "If you ever want to talk to me about anything, I'm here for you." When you know they need your undivided attention, give it to them as soon as possible. Listen and validate their thoughts and feelings.

CONVERSE. Some people struggle with talking *at* their kids. Others struggle responding *to* their kids. Identify your struggle and practice talking *with* your kids. Listen to them and then respond to continue the conversation. Share and let them respond to continue the conversation. Allow the conversation to be a true exchange.

ASK YOUR KIDS. If you have older kids, ages nine and up, ask them how you encourage conversation or silence them. This one is risky, but could be a meaningful conversation that opens a whole new relational dynamic *if* you are ready to listen, hear, and offer what they say is a need.

LISTEN AND PRAY. Words flow from the heart. Listen to yourself. Try to hear how you talk to your kids and how they echo your voice. Name any rudeness, accusations, anything ugly. Rejoice in kindness and sincere questions. Ask God to make the words you speak to your kids expressions of love.

TAKE RESPONSIBILITY. When you make mistakes, as we all do, take responsibility for your actions. Apologize to your kids and ask them to forgive you. If this is difficult for you, ask Jesus to help you make apologies and forgiveness a part of your family.

Chapter Seven

Conversation for Life

Our family lives in meaningful life-giving relationships. We laugh together. We share life together as parents and kids with responsibilities and privileges. Conversations carry us, but it was not always this way.

One night, we were all in the kitchen. With three young children and a strained marriage, I was weary to the point of defeat. You could feel the tension in the room. I could not tell you what one of the boys said, but I vividly recall my husband's indignant response, "Why do you let them talk to you that way?"

"You do," I replied, "Why wouldn't they?"

Soon after that brief exchange, we spent a year in marital counseling. I begged God to replace the angst in our home with joy. A few years later our oldest son shared with me something that happened at church. He had been asked to write something God had done in his heart—how things were before God intervened and how things were after God intervened. He wrote one thing down that he shared, but he confided in me the first thought that came to his mind. "We used to fight in our home. Now we laugh." I wept with joy. God had heard my cry. He transformed us from a family that lived life talking *at* each other—often unkindly—to a family that lives *a life shared* through meaningful conversation.

Start Where You Are

Conversations may be your new joy. Maintain your practice, keep the obstacles at bay, and explore new opportunities. Keep giving it a try. It is a daily choice to love those we live with through our openness to conversation.

Conversations may seem like a dream to you. You may realize the obstacles are many and the practice of conversation has not yet begun. You may bark more than talk in your home. You may live with the understanding that what you thought was a conversation, in reality, is you talking *at* your kids or listening without a response.

Wherever you are as a family, choose to live *a life shared*. Start where you are. There is no other place to begin. Confess your sin and ask forgiveness. Tackle one obstacle. Embrace one opportunity. Beg our good Father in heaven to bring victory where defeat looms. Cry out to Him for pure love for each one in your household. Start your conversation with Him. Let Him attend to you. He will show you the way day-by-day. Simply start where you are. It is never too early. It is never too late.

Never Too Early

It is never too early to begin a conversation with your kids. Practice may not ever make perfect, but the practice of conversation does lend itself to a relational dynamic that blesses our families. We did not bring home our newborn babies and wait to talk to them until they could talk. We began sharing life with them from the moment we held them in our arms. We called them by name. We told them about their hands and their toes. When we gave them time to hear our voice, and space to respond with a gaze or coo, we began our very first conversations.

The gentle father explaining to his toddler that accidents happen, as he cleans up dropped toys, continues the conversation. When his little one points and grunts, or even cries because his snack is spilled, dad can offer empathy in his response, "It is sad when our snack spills." This is a conversation. It is brief and can feel one-sided, but it is a conversation—a true exchange between parent and child.

Never Too Late

Established communication patterns are challenging to change, but not impossible. The parent, who answers for their child, can learn to encourage their child to find their own voice and develop a sense of *self* as a person. The parent, who talks *at* their children, can recognize their behavior and learn to talk *with* their child. Younger kids tend to be forgiving more quickly. Older kids are more conditioned, but will respond when we have proven ourselves to be truly open to conversation in a new way. Conversation as a true exchange can be established at any time.

After eighteen years, one mother and son had a pivotal conversation.

"I knew for many years I had issues with anger," the mother confessed. "I thought it was my circumstances—having a child with a difficult personality, too much stress, and three kids in three years. I was aware it was damaging. I prayed and cried for deliverance. I finally decided it was the best I could do. Then, I visited someone who had also been an uptight, stressed-out parent. This visit was different. She was different. She was gentle and kind. I asked her what happened, and she said she realized she had to change if she wanted anything to change."

"On the drive home, I prayed, *Lord, I will do whatever it takes.* Then it hit me. All the advice I had heard for years could not sink in because I had not been ready to pay the price to walk in love, be gentle, and kind. Finally, I was ready."

When she returned home, she took her oldest to lunch and humbly confessed her sins against him.

"I know I'm hard, Momma. I probably deserved it," he replied.

"No, you didn't deserve it," she explained through tears.

He had just graduated from high school and was moving away.

"If you need to go, go, but please don't go because you can't live with me," she said.

He stayed for ten more months. The relationship did not change overnight.

"My regret for what I had done to the kids was paralyzing," she recalled. "I hated myself for what I had done. I hated myself for my behavior. Then, I hated them for making me that way. Then, I hated myself that I blamed them."

When this mom forgave herself, the cycle unraveled. The history was still there, but they could finally live *a life shared.* She learned to love each child as they needed, and she let them love her in turn.

"If I had not become approachable," she told me, "we would have never shared life. I always wanted our relationship to be more. They felt like *I'm never good enough.* I made them feel that way. Who would want to be with someone that made you feel that way?"

Today, she and each child continue to welcome one another in a life that is truly shared. Regrets that once paralyzed her have been redeemed. It is never too late to live *a life shared* with our kids through meaningful conversation.

A Life Shared

When our kids are young, the conversation is about the discovery of their world. When they grow a bit older, the conversation is more of an exchange, as you share what you know with one another. When they enter the tween years, they begin the transition of discovering their world for themselves. Conversation changes as they require you to listen a great deal. At every age, we can be available to listen and respond. This will bless the relationship. Our family has chosen to adopt several practices over the years to encourage meaningful conversations. These practices remain intentionally consistent in our family.

Our family has conversation around the dinner table, on the road, over chores, and more. We talk about our days and ourselves. I hope you made discoveries and began practices from "Your Turn To Share" and "Give It A Try" for your family to share life through conversation. Meaningful conversation blesses your family, but the blessings extend far beyond that. Kids who share life with their family can have meaningful conversations with others outside their family. The ability to have a conversation with others is vital for living a life shared. It is not only vital for your relationship, but for your child's relationships throughout her life. Your child's skill with meaningful conversations can even impact the generations to come.

"I love how your kids can actually have a conversation! They ask me how I am and listen to my answer." I hear this all the time whether it is about my *quiet one* or my *sweet one*. The practice of conversation in our home empowers our kids to share life with others—to see them, to hear them, and to respond to them. This is not unique to my family. I get to have conversations with kids of all ages, as our family shares life with others. The college students I see and talk with in worship learned conversation across generations. It blesses us as we share life week after week.

As They Grow Older

Recently, I asked my almost thirteen-year-old if he thought kids wanted to share their lives with their parents.

"Maybe," he muttered with a look of almost disgust on his face.

"Why wouldn't they?" I asked.

"Sometimes, you just want things to be private," he began. And then, my quiet kid who suggested kids don't want to share life carried on about himself for at least five minutes. I smiled and listened. He said one thing but meant another.

As they grow older, their initial response is often a feeling or reaction, and not always reflective of their true heart. They test us. They feel us out before they take the risk of sharing. When we give them space, they think out loud and share. Will we really listen? Do we really care? Do we encourage conversation? Our older kids need to make sure. Once conversation is a relational dynamic, you will know, because they will come to you to share their life and heart with you. As they grow older, they may withdraw from time to time, mutter one-word replies, and moan at your existence. But the relationship is not lost; it is merely changing. Keep engaging them, listening to them, and being available for them.

Conversation for Life

I am blessed to have experienced the power of meaningful

conversation during my own lifetime. While we all stumble at times, my parents taught me by their example. I began this book with a conversation about cancer. My dad's cancer went away, only to come back. We lived that pattern for three years. Eventually, in two short months, he went from living with routine treatments, to the hospital discharging him to Hospice care. One month later, he could not talk on the phone. His voice was too weak. The last discernable words he spoke to me were, "How's your book?" He always said I would write books. We had had that conversation for years. Those words have carried me through the writing of this book. His words echoed in my ears, and his confidence in me as a writer prodded me onward when the task felt too great.

Some days I am saddened by the loss of my father. The boys know it, but I tell them anyway because it is good for us to remember.

"I miss Papaw today. He would have been working in the greenhouse. I wonder how big his seedlings would be," I explain. They smile and talk about his grand garden and wonderful dinners.

Some days something happens he would have loved. We talk about how—if he were still here—we would call him to tell him about the wrestling match victory, the welding project, and the book. We cannot call him, but he is a part of our conversations for life, and those conversations bring life—even after death—in the most beautiful ways.

My mom has been my rock—steady and always present. My teen years were hard on her as I embraced risky behavior. I don't remember specific conversations growing up, but I remember I could talk to my mom. She was available, even when I was an obnoxious, young Christian. The dramatic change in my life was not one I traversed gracefully, yet she welcomed me to share life with her again and again.

In recent years, we have had some risky conversations—the kind where I have said, "When you do this, it is hurtful. I know you don't mean to hurt me, so I wanted you to know." She listened, heard, and responded in love with regret and willingness to change. I could take the risk of talking with her about my hurts in our relationship because conversation is a relational dynamic we have embraced for years. She is safe. I know she loves me and chooses us.

Our dream has always been to have *a life shared* with our kids, and meaningful conversations help bring that dream to life. We don't have to always get it right. I don't. My parents didn't. All we have to do is choose to be the parent whose actions communicate to our kids, "I am for you. I see you. I hear you. You are safe with me." By the grace of God and our commitment to bless our kids as their parents, our dreams come true day by day. May we live *a life shared* and have endless conversations for generations to come.

Jesus, You are with us. Help us live a life
shared with You and our kids day-by-day.

Your Turn To Share

Chapter six's "Give It A Try" invited you to encourage conversation with your kids. What was one thing you tried? How did it go?

This chapter includes personal stories. Was there anything from those stories you found surprising, confusing, inspiring, or encouraging?

How have your prayers and actions shaped your dream of a life with your kids as adults as you have worked through this book?

What is God showing you about yourself? What are you learning about your need to have *meaningful* conversations with your kids?

God hears us and offers us life abundant in Jesus. How have you experienced His grace to transform you and your family, so you can share life through meaningful conversation?

As you reflect on the chapters and themes of this book, what stands out as an answer to your hopes and prayers? What practices have you begun and plan to continue?

Give It A Try!

NAME AND PRAISE. Name life-giving changes in your heart and family. Give God thanks for His care for you and your family. Rejoice with a friend or share with a group.

WELCOME AND ENGAGE. Choose to live your life so that your actions let your kids know, "I am for you. I see you. I hear you. You are safe with me."

START WHERE YOU ARE. Reflect on where you are after reading this book. Name ways you will choose to live *a life shared* with your family through meaningful conversation.

To order more copies of

A LIFE SHARED

Order online at:

• www.CertaPublishing/ALifeShared

• or call 1-855-77-CERTA

Also available on Amazon.com